NATIONS OF NORTH AMERICA

SIOUX

THOMAS KINGSLEY TROUPE

A Lighthouse Book
SEAHORSE
PUBLISHING

Teaching Tips for Caregivers:

As a caregiver, you can help your child succeed in school by giving them a strong foundation in language and literacy skills and a desire to learn by reading.

Reading for pleasure and interest will help your child to develop reading skills and will provide the opportunity to practice these skills in meaningful ways. Use the following strategies.

- Encourage the student to read independently at home.
- Encourage the student to practice reading aloud.
- Encourage activities that require reading.
- Establish a regular reading time.
- Have the student write questions about what they read.

Teaching Tips for Teachers:

Engage students throughout the reading process by asking questions.
Sample responses are provided.

Before Reading

- **What do I know about the Sioux?**
  I know that Crazy Horse was a great Sioux chief.
  I know that the Sioux defeated General Custer in the Battle of Little Bighorn.
- **What do I want to learn about this topic?**
  I want to learn why the Sioux had to fight so many battles.
  I want to learn how the Sioux hunted and used bison.

During Reading

- **I'm curious to know...**
  I'm curious to know more about how horses helped the Sioux and made life easier for them.
  I'm curious to know at what age Sioux boys were allowed to go hunting.
- **How is this like something I already know?**
  I have read about other tribes that lived on the Great Plains.
  I have visited the Black Hills or seen pictures of them.

After Reading

- **What was the author trying to teach me?**
  I think the author was trying to teach me that the Sioux fought hard to protect their land.
  I think the author was trying to teach me that the Sioux used all the gifts from nature to survive.
- **How did the photographs and captions help me understand more?**
  I learned what tepees and other Sioux creations look like.
  I learned where the Great Plains are in the United States.

TABLE OF CONTENTS

On the cover: Sioux men on horseback wear eagle feather war bonnets in 1905 on the Great Plains. Traditionally, war bonnets could only be worn by important chiefs and warriors. Men earned feathers for acts of great bravery in battle. The number of feathers showed a Sioux warrior's rank in the tribe.

CHAPTER 1: THE SIOUX NATION

Women scrape **bison** skins. They will trade them for corn and other supplies.

Tribal leaders on the Great **Plains** join forces to fight and win the Battle of Little Bighorn.

Friends gather over the weekend in a sweat lodge. Inside, they say a traditional prayer.

Young people take a road trip to visit the Black Hills. They join the effort to return the mountains to their tribe.

What do these stories have in common? They are all part of the proud history of the people of the Sioux Nation.

CHAPTER 2: SIOUX HOMELANDS

The Sioux are one of the largest and oldest Native American tribes. People from the Sioux Nation have lived in North America for thousands of years.

REGIONS

Long ago, the Sioux lived near the Great Lakes. But wars with other tribes made them move west. When Spanish invaders brought horses to North America, the Sioux learned to ride. This helped them travel.

The word *Sioux* is short for *Nadouessioux*, which means "little snakes." The name was given to the Sioux by their enemies in the Ojibwe tribe.

Sioux Homeland

The Sioux became **nomadic** people who followed and hunted bison. Their lands stretched across the northern Great Plains. As they moved, they split into three groups called the Lakota, the Dakota, and the Nakota. All three names mean "**allies**."

Sioux homelands on the Great Plains are now parts of Colorado, Kansas, Montana, Nebraska, North Dakota, South Dakota, and Wyoming.

THE STRUGGLE FOR LAND

Life became difficult for the Sioux when white **settlers** moved onto their land on the Great Plains. The Sioux needed their land and the bison herds to survive.

Sioux tribes tried to make peace with the United States government. They signed **treaties** and agreed to give up some of their land. But settlers kept coming. They wanted to build roads, railroads, and forts on Sioux lands. This led to many battles.

Sioux warriors battle U.S. troops near Rosebud Creek in Montana.

The Black Hills in South Dakota and Wyoming are very special to the Sioux people. The Lakota Sioux call the mountains there Paha Sapa and believe they are the center of the universe. Many in the Sioux Nation are still fighting for ownership of this area today.

Then, gold was discovered in the Black Hills. Thousands of miners and settlers ignored Sioux land rights. The Sioux had to fight to defend their homes.

CHAPTER 3: TRADITIONAL SIOUX WAYS OF LIFE

Long ago, Sioux people lived across the Great Plains. The land provided what they needed.

FOOD

The Sioux were mostly hunters. But some grew crops like beans, corn, and squash. Since they moved around a lot, the Sioux used what they could find. They gathered wild roots, turnips, potatoes, berries, and fruits.

Bison and buffalo are often confused. Water buffalo and Cape buffalo live in South Asia and Africa. Bison are found in North America and some areas of Europe. In the 1800s, there were close to 60 million bison in North America. By 1889, there were only about 500 left, and bison were nearly extinct. The animals had been overhunted by settlers. Thankfully, work was done to protect bison. There are between 12,000 and 15,000 bison in the world today.

The Sioux hunted deer, elk, bear, and wild turkey. But their biggest food source was bison. The people moved with the bison herds. In addition to food, bison hunts provided **hides** for making tepees, clothing, and tools. Every part of the bison was used.

SHELTER

Traditionally, the Sioux lived in simple homes called tepees (or tipis). The cone-shaped tents were made with long wooden poles. They were covered with animal skins. Tepees were easy to move when the people needed to travel for hunting.

The size of Sioux tepees changed when they began to use horses instead of traveling on foot. Since horses could carry more, tepees became larger.

A tepee offered protection from bad weather. It sheltered as many as ten people. A warm campfire burned inside.

Women set up and repaired tepees. Each cover was made from more than a dozen hides. Together with the poles, a tepee could weigh more than 500 pounds (225 kilograms). Many tepees were decorated with colorful symbols and pictures of animals.

LANGUAGE

The Sioux language is part of the Siouan language family. Siouan-speaking tribes can be found all over North America. Because the Sioux Nation is divided into different groups, the Sioux language has different **dialects**. Using their language allows Sioux people to express their religion, history, and beliefs in ways that other languages cannot.

In the past, Sioux people were experts at using a type of sign language. This American Indian Sign Language, or "Hand Talk," allowed them to communicate with many other tribes.

For a time, it was against the law to use Sioux languages. Children were taken from their families and sent away to schools to learn English. But Sioux languages survived. Today, many people learn to speak and write in the Dakota, Lakota, and Nakota dialects.

For nearly 40 years, Native American children were taken from their families and sent to live at the Carlisle Indian Industrial School in Pennsylvania.

FAMILY AND SOCIETY

Long ago, Sioux women prepared food, made medicine from local plants, and helped prepare bison hides and other items to trade. Children did chores, played games, and learned to ride horses from a young age. Sioux men were excellent hunters and warriors. They provided meat and protected their families.

Groups of families traveled together. If needed, they could move every day along with the bison. One member of the group acted as chief. Several groups might unite under one leader. Decisions were often made by a tribal council.

Women dried bison meat to make jerky. This important food could be packed for a journey, and it was good to eat for more than a year.

White people first brought horses to North America. The Sioux soon learned to ride and breed them. They depended on horses for hunting and traveling. Sioux people respected their animals and took good care of them.

CHAPTER 4: TRADITIONAL SIOUX CREATIONS

Hundreds of years ago, Sioux people made most of the things they needed. They used wild plants, animal hides, and other natural materials.

BOWLS AND POTS

Traditionally, the Sioux carved animal heads on wooden bowls. These were used for ceremonies and feasts. They also made beautiful pottery with red clay from the Black Hills. Their creations had colorful patterns and shapes that can still be seen in artwork today.

Quillwork is a traditional Sioux art form. Porcupine quills were softened, dyed, and woven through clothing and other items in colorful patterns. Quillwork was later replaced with beadwork.

CLOTHING

Long ago, bison hides were decorated and worn. Paints and dyes came from wild plants. Women often wore skins with brightly colored shapes. Artwork on the men's hides might tell a story about a hunt or a raid.

WEAPONS

As hunters and warriors long ago, the Sioux depended on weapons to survive. They made bows and arrows for hunting and for battle. They learned to fire arrows on horseback. The Sioux also made a variety of clubs and knives.

Spears were the best weapons for hunting bison. The Sioux made them from long poles with a sharp pointed piece attached to the end. They would ride alongside the animals on their horses and throw the spears. Bison hunting was dangerous! It required courage and skill.

Wood bows and arrows were custom-made for each hunter. Early arrowheads were bone or stone. Later, the Sioux traded for steel. Bowstrings were made from a bison's tendons, or sinew.

A bear claw necklace was a traditional symbol of strength for Sioux warriors. Wearing it was said to bring protection and good health.

CHAPTER 5: SIOUX LEADERS

Throughout history, great Sioux leaders have united their people and defended their way of life.

Sioux chief Red Cloud went to Washington, D.C., to speak out about the mistreatment of Native Americans.

SITTING BULL (1831 TO 1890)

Sitting Bull was a Sioux chief who helped unite the tribes of the Great Plains. Together with the Arapaho and the Cheyenne, the Sioux battled with the U.S. government to keep land that had been promised to them.

The U.S. Army wanted to force the Sioux out of the Black Hills. Many U.S. troops were sent to fight the Native Americans, led in part by Sitting Bull. Though the Sioux won many battles, they couldn't win the war. Settlers kept moving in, and bison were becoming extinct. Hungry and outnumbered, Sitting Bull and his people had no choice but to surrender.

Sitting Bull

CRAZY HORSE (1841 TO 1877)

Crazy Horse was a warrior and chief to the Oglala Sioux. He led his people to **resist** the U.S. government from forcing them onto **reservations**.

At the Battle of Little Bighorn in 1876, Crazy Horse, Sitting Bull, and their followers stopped U.S. **reinforcements** from arriving. This helped thousands of Native American fighters kill U.S. General George Custer and all 600 of his men. This event became known as Custer's Last Stand.

In this painting, George Custer is shown kneeling on the left. He and his soldiers are fighting Native Americans on horseback.

Crazy Horse fought for many years. Finally, in 1877, he led over one thousand hungry followers to surrender to the U.S. at a reservation in Nebraska. He died soon after.

Crazy Horse refused to be photographed. But a giant sculpture being carved into the Black Hills will let many people see the face of this brave leader. The Crazy Horse Memorial was started decades ago and is still not finished.

CHAPTER 6: THE SIOUX PEOPLE TODAY

More than 150,000 Sioux people live in the U.S. today. Many live in North Dakota, South Dakota, Minnesota, Nebraska, and Montana. Some Sioux people live in Canada.

Native American riders lasso cows on the Lower Brule Sioux Tribal Reservation in South Dakota.

Reservations are like separate countries within the U.S. They have their own governments, police, and services. People who live there are members of their tribes and citizens of the United States.

RESERVATIONS

Though they can live anywhere, many Sioux people choose to live on reservations. Sioux reservations stretch across 3,000 miles (4,828 kilometers) of the U.S. One is the Pine Ridge Indian Reservation in South Dakota. It is the second-largest reservation in the U.S.

HONORING THEIR HERITAGE

Modern Sioux people have ordinary modern lives. But they remember their tribal heritage. Children are taught Sioux languages. Many people participate in traditional ceremonies. They learn to hunt and create artwork like their proud ancestors did.

Families gather at celebrations and **powwows** each year. There are art shows, traditional music, and dance competitions. These tribal festivals help people remember that they are part of the proud Sioux Nation of North America.

Young Sioux people gather at the annual United Tribes Powwow, where hundreds of Native American dancers celebrate their cultures.

The Sioux sweat lodge ceremony, or inipi, takes place inside a circular lodge. Water is poured over heated rocks, and steam fills the air. There is singing and praying as people begin to sweat. They invite healing spirits to visit. Over three hours, the door is opened three times. The fourth time, the people come out. Their bodies and spirits feel reborn.

GLOSSARY

allies (AL-eyes): people, groups, or countries who are on the same side or who are working together to complete a goal; friends

bison (BYE-suhn): large animals that are found in western North America and that have big, shaggy heads, a humped back, and short horns

dialects (DYE-uh-lekts): ways that a language is spoken in a particular place or among a particular group of people; different forms of the same language

hides (hides): skins of animals that are used to make leather

nomadic (noh-MAD-ik): traveling from place to place instead of living in the same place all the time

plains (playnz): large, flat areas of land

powwows (POU-wouz): gatherings for Native Americans that are organized for social or ceremonial reasons; may include traditional singing, dancing, and drumming

reinforcements (ree-in-FORS-muhnts): extra troops sent to strengthen an army; people who come to help or support

reservations (rez-ur-VAY-shuhnz): areas of land set aside by the government for ownership by Native American tribes

resist (ri-ZIST): to fight back, oppose, struggle against, or refuse to accept

settlers (SET-luhrz): people who make their homes in a new place and who sometimes invade and oppress Indigenous peoples who originally lived there

treaties (TREE-teez): agreements between two nations

INDEX

COMPREHENSION QUESTIONS

1. In what battle was General Custer defeated?
   a. Battle of Falling Rocks
   b. Battle of Little Bighorn
   c. Battle of 1876

2. True or False: Buffalo and bison are the same animal.

3. Where are Sioux homelands?
   a. the northern plains
   b. the eastern swamps
   c. the southwestern deserts

4. True or False: The Black Hills are a special place for Sioux people.

5. Crazy Horse refused to ______.
   a. give up his horse
   b. be photographed
   c. fish and hunt

Answer Key: 1. b 2. False 3. a 4. True 5. b

ABOUT THE AUTHOR

Thomas Kingsley Troupe is the author of over 200 books for young readers. When he's not writing, he enjoys reading, playing video games, and investigating haunted places with the Twin Cities Paranormal Society. Otherwise, he's probably taking a nap or something. Thomas lives in Woodbury, Minnesota, with his two sons.

Written by: Thomas Kingsley Troupe
Design by: Under the Oaks Media
Series Development: James Earley
Editor: Kim Thompson

Photo credits: Everett Collection: cover; Everett Collection: p. 1; LOC: p. 4; LOC: p. 4; arindambanerjee: p. 5; Iker Zabaleta: p. 5; LOC: p. 6; LOC: p. 8; macrowildlife: p. 9; Wollertz: p. 9; LOC: p. 9; SamanthaZurbrick: p. 10; LOC: p. 12; LOC: p. 13; Everett Collection: p. 14; LOC: p. 15; LOC: p. 15; LOC: p. 16; Everett Collection: p. 17; Raisa Nastukova: p. 18; Shiiko Alexander: p. 19; LOC: p. 20; Everett Collection: p. 21; LOC: p. 21; LOC: p. 22; LOC: p. 23; LOC: p. 24; Glenn Perreira: p. 25; LOC: p. 25; Joseph Sohm: p. 26; Sopotnicki: p. 27; Pierre Jean Durieu: p. 28; Photo Spirit: p. 29

Library of Congress PCN Data
Sioux / Thomas Kingsley Troupe
Nations of North America
ISBN 978-1-6389-7993-7 (hard cover)
ISBN 979-8-8873-5052-3 (paperback)
ISBN 979-8-8873-5111-7 (EPUB)
ISBN 979-8-8873-5170-4 (eBook)
Library of Congress Control Number: 2022943809

Printed in the United States of America.

Seahorse Publishing Company
seahorsepub.com

Published in the United States
Seahorse Publishing
PO Box 771325
Coral Springs, FL 33077

SEAHORSE PUBLISHING